The Gospel According to Pixar

The Gospel According to Pixar

A Study Guide for Families, Churches and Individuals
Edited by Todd Brewer and David Zahl

Mockingbird Ministries
100 W. Jefferson St
Charlottesville, VA 22902
www.mbird.com

Table of Contents

Introduction

We developed this series to help families, churches, and individuals connect Christianity with people's everyday lives, using the powerful illustrations found in the films made by Pixar Animation Studios. Over the past fifteen years, Pixar has produced a remarkable body of work, films that speak in fresh terms about the reality of life and the complexities of the human heart – and make us laugh while doing so. We see these films as much more than children's fare; we see them as the closest thing we have to modern-day folk tales. And like many great folk tales, Pixar uses monsters, fish, toys, and other fantastical characters to touch winsomely on universal, and, therefore, Gospel-related themes.

For Pixar, what makes a good story is character development. Rather than the dramatic events themselves, the characters drive the plot, as they are changed by who and what they encounter. Their adventures, while always entertaining, serve more as interruptions in the protagonists' lives, i.e., the means by which internal conflicts are set in motion. Consequently, every Pixar movie features characters who are acted upon and transformed by some external force or event. That Christian themes would emerge out of this dynamic should come as no surprise.

In making these connections we by no means wish to imply that Pixar films are overtly or exclusively religious in nature. They are works of art, and to reduce their dimension would do them a great disservice. Our aim is simply to identify where the stories themselves resonate with, and illustrate, a Christian understanding of life.

Using This Guide

This guide is designed to be versatile, both in terms of audience and setting. Since so many young people have grown up watching Pixar films, a youth ministry is perhaps the most natural context. Pixar films already occupy a cherished place in young people's hearts; the most difficult work of this series has already been done.

Yet Pixar excels at making films suitable for all-ages – they are the quintessential "kids' films that parents love" – and we hope that this series has a similarly broad scope. It can just as easily be used at home, for example at "Family Movie Nights," where families watch a movie together, and then discuss.

Better yet, we recommend using this guide with older audiences. Like all great art, these movies operate on multiple levels and speak to the major questions of human life: the elusiveness and power of love, the pain of death, the reality of suffering and fear, the hope of belonging, and the search for purpose and identity, to name just a few. We guarantee that you will be surprised by the response, not to mention the breadth of the films' popularity. At points, those using this guide with younger audiences may even need to simplify its language.

Finally, *The Gospel According to Pixar* is meant to function as a publication in its own right. By no means does it require a group. Individuals of all ages, both the casual fan and the Pixar connoisseur, are encouraged to read it simply as a commentary on the films.

Format

We hope that these outlines will allow individuals, churches, para-church organizations, and small groups to offer *The Gospel According to Pixar* (TGATP) in their communities. To that end, we have constructed eight sessions, each of which centers around a full movie. You don't have to use all of the sessions; they work independently as well as in sequence. Feel free to pick and choose based on your context and time frame.

In preparing to lead a session, we recommend first watching the entire film, even if you have seen it before. Next, reading the entire talk is a must. Some of them are lengthier than others and may need to be pared down for presentation. None of them cover every redemptive aspect or possible theological connection of the film at hand. We encourage you to explore those elements of the film that connect most with you personally, and build your talk from there, incorporating personal, real-life illustrations that parallel the themes in the talk/film.

What follows are two variations of how TGATP has been run in the past.

Option One: presenting TGATP over a series of two-hour weekly meetings, thus an eight-week program. It can also be used for week-long retreats, with one or two sessions per day. In the weekly meeting format, each session could proceed as follows:

* Welcome and opening prayer: 2 min
* Dinner (Pizza is tried and true, but feel free to be creative): 30-45 min
* Lecture on the movie (with selected clips): 45-60 min
* Large group discussion: 20-30 min

Using the clips indicated in each talk, the whole evening should not take more than two hours. If you have young families that might be interested in attending, we suggest you provide childcare.

Option Two: presenting TGATP over a series of three-hour meetings, or "movie nights," where an entire film is screened each time. This is perfect for a Friday or Saturday evening event. Plus, showing the entire film eliminates the technological difficulties of arranging the exact movie clips. The films all have running times of roughly 100 minutes, so an on-time start is imperative. In this scenario, each session could proceed as follows:

- Welcome and opening prayer: 2 min
- Short intro to the film: 6 min
- Primer Questions: 2 min. *We've provided a few examples at the end of each outline, which double as Discussion Questions. You are encouraged to come up with your own! With younger audiences, we have found that some basic rehashing of the plot can be helpful.*
- Play movie and eat dinner: 100 min
- Bathroom/drink refill break: 10 min
- Lecture on the film: 30-40 min
- Large group discussion: 20-30 min

Please note, since video and audio clips are essential to this material, some kind of playback/screening capability is required. Video editing and slideshow programs could be used in advance, or someone can cue the videos while the talk is given. Do not try to give the talk without the video. Much of the power lies in the images themselves.

Finally, thank you for your interest in *The Gospel According to Pixar*. We hope you find it fun, thought-provoking and helpful. "To infinity and beyond!"

Contributors: Todd Brewer, Nick Lannon, Lauren Larkin, Bonnie Zahl & David Zahl
Special thanks to Liz Edrington, Cate West Zahl & Aaron Zimmerman

WALL-E: **Post-Apocalyptic Robot Love**

Synopsis

The world has become an uninhabitable garbage dump. Humans have relocated to outer space, leaving robots like our protagonist WALL-E to clean up the world. One day, another robot lands on Earth. Her name is EVE. The humans in space have sent her to find signs of life on Earth – as an indication that the planet may finally be ready for resettling. WALL-E soon falls in love with EVE, showing her his prized possessions. As a sign of his love, WALL-E offers EVE his new-found treasure: a green shoot of a plant. Having found what she was looking for, EVE involuntarily "locks down" and waits for the space ship to collect her. WALL-E is confused by her sudden non-responsiveness, but devotes himself to caring for her in her inactive state, eventually following her and stowing away on the humans' space ship. On board, he finds a ship full of overweight people driving armchairs, talking to each other only via video screens and eating their food out of giant Slurpee cups. Computers run the ship, keeping the humans alive and pacified. When WALL-E arrives, he single-mindedly pursues EVE and helps her complete her directive, despite opposition from the head robot, the Autopilot, who seeks to maintain power by preventing the spaceship's return to Earth.

WALL-E's One-Way Love for EVE and His Sense of Wonder

The most poignant aspect of the film has to do with the ripple effect of WALL-E's one-way love towards EVE. Furthermore, in his love for her, he demonstrates a tremendous sense of wonder at the world. This is what breaks EVE (and many others) out of their programmed existence. This talk explores the impact and nature of WALL-E's love by looking at his relationship to EVE, and how EVE, the Captain, the other humans, and the other robots change as WALL-E enters their lives.

EVE – Play 27:20 to 34:12

WALL-E's appreciation for beauty (despite the very un-beautiful world around him) is evident in his little home, especially his enchantment with the video he shows EVE. WALL-E recognizes that all he wants in the world is EVE. He loves her and just wants to hold her hand.

1) WALL-E is entirely and completely devoted to EVE. He shields her from the harsh weather. They watch the sunset together. WALL-E makes EVE's well-being his directive even to the point of being launched into space. Yet EVE is relatively unresponsive to WALL-E (both before and after her "lock down"). Her mind is focused only on her directive. Has she reciprocated WALL-E's love at all? No. She wants to send WALL-E home so that he does not get in the way of completing her mission of delivering the plant. She doesn't want him around.

   a) **Play 55:15 to 56:54** – Stop when EVE says "Directive"

The Ripples of WALL-E's Love

Before we discuss the change of heart that takes place vis-à-vis EVE, let's look at how WALL-E affects some of the other characters in the film. In a frequently humorous way, WALL-E's love for EVE disrupts the status quo on the wider ship, breaking people out of destructive patterns and leading them to experience joy and wonder.

The Captain and the People – Play 39:30 to 42:57 and 1:00:40 to 1:02:07

1) When WALL-E lands on the spaceship, he finds its population of overweight people to be completely disinterested in actually interacting *with* each other. They live their lives on floating deck chairs, talking to each other through video screens. They never actually look at one another. When WALL-E accidentally breaks one woman's chair so that her video screen no longer works, the lady begins to see the world beyond herself. She begins to appreciate beauty, and she begins to reach out to those around her. She can't contain her wonder at the world she is seeing for the first time.

2) The hope WALL-E brings for returning to Earth inspires within the Captain of the ship a curiosity and wonder about what Earth is like. WALL-E jolts the Captain out of his monotonous existence: for the first time in his life the Captain is amazed and in awe of something beyond his own existence, another ripple effect of WALL-E's loyal pursuit of EVE.

The Rogue Robots – Play 52:45 to 55:18

1) Not only does WALL-E disrupt the ordinary, boring lives of the humans, he also affects the other robots on the ship. There is a "Repair Ward" on the ship in which all the broken (i.e., crazy) robots have to remain and be fixed. In his concern for EVE, he accidentally frees them. One might think this would lead to utter chaos; however, we later see that in one of EVE and WALL-E's most desperate moments, these robots come to their aid. They are no longer "broken" or "useless" – they have a cause: to

help WALL-E and EVE bring the plant to its rightful destination. It is no stretch to see the parallels here with Jesus and the attraction he held for broken people like tax collectors, prostitutes, and sinners.

Play 1:05:12 to 1:05:55 and 1:13:43 to 1:15:52

EVE's Change of Heart

1) The past is revealed. She finally able to see everything that happened when she went into "lock down" mode. She slowly begins to realize that WALL-E has done more than just help her with her directive. EVE realizes that WALL-E loves her.

2) The One-Way Love of WALL-E (The most important part of the film!)

   a) While helping EVE complete her directive, WALL-E is severely injured. When she sees him in pain, her heart is touched. Instead of continuing to try to send him home, she decides to help him. In a single moment, her directive is subordinated to her love for WALL-E. Love allows EVE to see beyond her single-minded existence. She finds herself willing to give up her directive to save WALL-E. Or rather, her directive and saving WALL-E become the same thing.

   b) This is the crux of one-way love: WALL-E doesn't help EVE with her directive *so that she will love him*. He helps her because he loves her, period. There's no hint of manipulation, no hint of "if I show her love this way she will love me back." WALL-E loves EVE so much that her welfare is his only concern; he is entirely focused on her. As far as WALL-E is concerned, EVE is the most important person/robot in the world.

c) This love transforms EVE: she changes from being inwardly driven (by her directive) to being outwardly driven, by love for WALL-E. As she is loved, she becomes able to love; she becomes selfless. And look at the ripple effects of WALL-E's love! Look at the change in the people, the captain, the "broken" robots. They all become more than what they were.

One-Way Love in the Bible

1) Read about Zacchaeus in Luke 19:1-10. The story of WALL-E and his one-way love is a sign-post that points to God's one-way love in Jesus. Look at how Jesus interacts with Zacchaeus.

   a) Zacchaeus served the Roman empire as a tax collector. He was seen by his Jewish contemporaries as a traitor for consorting with the occupying force. Though he was a wealthy man, his fellow Jews saw him as an outcast. Jesus comes to town and declares that he wants to eat at Zacchaeus' house. Jesus enters into Zacchaeus' life and extends love and acceptance to a man who was judged by others (for good reason).

   b) In response, Zacchaeus is transformed: instead of acting as the chief tax collector, Zacchaeus gives half of his possessions to the poor and extends generosity towards people.

2) 1 John 3:16a: *"This is how we know what love is: Jesus Christ laid down his life for us."*

   a) The most amazing instance of one-way love in the Bible is Jesus' death. Like WALL-E, Jesus gave up everything for the benefit of others – you and me. But Jesus did much more than WALL-E. He sacrificed his life not for something as innocuous as a robot's "directive"; he sacrificed his life for us, even while we were still sinners (Rom 5:8).

3) The rejuvenation of Earth that we see as the film (and credits) unfold underlines this sense of new life, *a lá* Psalm 84:6: *"As they pass through the valley of Baca, they make it a place of springs."*

   a) The way WALL-E breaks people out of their ordinary way of life and causes them to look beyond themselves also reminds us of how the spirit of God revives and renews people. Everything that WALL-E touches is transformed. Something new grows that is life-giving and wonderful and refreshing.

   b) WALL-E restores a sense of wonder in people; they see the world again for the first time. *"Jesus said: 'Let the little children come to me, and do not hinder them, for the kingdom of heaven belongs to such as these'"* (Matthew 19:14). WALL-E helped those around him become like little children again.

Discussion and Primer Questions

1. What about WALL-E sets him apart from other robots? Why does he collect things?

2. Can you think of a time when you were broken out of a pattern or funk? What broke you out of it? Have you ever had a "directive" that gave you tunnel-vision?

3. Have there been any times in your life when you've been able to show someone this kind of one-way love? Have you ever received it from someone? Why do you think it's so rare?

4. WALL-E restores a sense of wonder in the people (and robots) around him. Can you think of a time when you've had your sense of wonder restored? What was it like?

The Incredibles: (Secret) Identity and the Problem of Being a "Super"

Synopsis

Bob Parr and his wife, Helen, used to be among the world's greatest crime fighters, saving lives and battling evil on a daily basis as Mr. Incredible and Elastigirl. Fifteen years later, they have been forced to adopt civilian identities and retreat to the suburbs where they live "normal" lives with their three kids, Violet, Dash, and Jack-Jack. Itching to get back into action, Bob gets his chance when a mysterious communication summons him to a remote island for a top-secret assignment. He soon discovers that it will take a super family effort to rescue the world from total destruction.

Play 0:00 to 9:15

Introduction

The movie begins with a newsclip of Frozone talking about identity. The question "who am I?" occupies, and pre-occupies, much of our lives. It is also a question that drives *The*

Incredibles. Superheroes, after all, lead double lives. Who are they? The hero? Or the "mild-mannered alter ego"? What happens when they are told they cannot be "super"? And how do their identities as superheroes impact those without super-powers?

Identity in *The Incredibles*

We find at least three different approaches to the question "Who am I?," in Mr. Incredible, Syndrome and Elastigirl, respectively.

Mr. Incredible/Bob Parr

1) He is forbidden to be who he is, a superhero, which means he can't use his natural abilities. He is forced to work a boring job as an insurance adjuster.

   a) This prohibition creates resentment (of his boss, of his car) and rebellion (illegal acting out, like using a police scanner to catch bad guys), not to mention marital strife.

      i) **Play clip of Bob's argument with Helen from 24:15 to 26:50.**

   b) When he receives a top-secret mission and resumes his superhero identity, something changes. Affirmation and love from the outside (Mirage) have a significant impact on how he feels about himself. His newfound freedom from the prohibition results in:

      i) Rebirth – **Play montage from 41:25 to 42:45.** The freedom to be "who he is" brings Mr. Incredible new life. It births goodness, creativity, energy, and happiness at home. He becomes a better father and husband.

(a) This is true in our own lives as well. Feelings about oneself manifest themselves in actions. Goodness begins on the inside and works its way outward, not the other way around. (The flipside of what Jesus describes in Mark 7:14-23).

ii) But this sort of affirmation also fosters self-absorption. Mr. Incredible becomes completely preoccupied by himself, by his abilities and by his importance. He is unable to see or love those around him. He lies to his wife to cover up his new life.

c) The turning point for Mr. Incredible is when he finds out that his wife and children have been killed. He is forced to confront the consequences of his self-involvement and in that moment, he gives up on his identity as such. In this vacuum, the love of his family breathes new life and strength into him.

Syndrome/Buddy

1) He has tried to make himself into a superhero, so that he'll feel "good enough." He believes, on some deep level, that in order to be of value he must be super. His is a life based on what a Christian theologian might call "works righteousness," of trying to make himself powerful on his own. Syndrome sees himself as a champion of self-reliance.

a) As the clip at the beginning shows us, Buddy's motivations are born out of a desire to get approval and love from Mr. Incredible. When he doesn't receive that approval – when he is *rejected as a boy* – his identity becomes reactive and takes a turn toward "the dark side." He'll do whatever it takes to prove himself and to beat/become Mr. Incredible and win the love of the world.

i) **Play the clip of Buddy/Syndrome's rationalization from 50:40 to 54:00.**

b) The not-good-enough-ness will never be satisfied or silenced. Syndrome leads a tortuous and hateful existence. It is not surprising that he is driven mad.

Elastigirl/Helen Parr (and the kids)

1) Unlike the men, Mrs. Parr's identity does not seem to be caught up in doing, at least not directly. To the extent that we see it, her identity exists in relation to her children and her husband.

    a) Her identity is derived from her role in the family, which is directly related to her desire for stability and control. She has suppressed her former self completely "for the sake of the family." But her desires *for* her family seem to conflict with their desires for themselves. As a result she is perceived as a law-giver, both by the children and by her husband: well-meaning but a bit of a killjoy, maternal yet tunnel-visioned, micro-managing and generally a bit fearful.

        i) It may not be justified, but her children's disobedience and her husband's deceit are a direct response to her identity as family law-giver. Her role as policewoman creates resentment.

    b) Elastigirl's love for her family ends up being the change agent in the film. The crisis between Bob and Syndrome forces her to give up control. It yanks her out of her personal inertia and fears – directly into the moment. She rescues the children who have disobeyed her and sacrifices herself for the husband that has deceived her.

        i) **Play clip of Helen saving the kids from 1:08:00 to 1:15:20.** We see an example of completely one-way provision and love – grace almost. She becomes a parachute and then a boat *a lá* the mother in the classic children's tale *The Runaway Bunny*.

(1) Jesus says in Luke 13:34: *"O Jerusalem, Jerusalem, you who kill the prophets and stone those sent to you, how often I have longed to gather your children together, as a hen gathers her chicks under her wings…"*

c) Helen forgives Violet. She gives, or imputes, an identity to her – "you will know." Her love gives both Violet and Dash confidence. Her love bestows identity on them. Her love also jars Mr. Incredible out of his self-centeredness.

Identity in the Bible

1) The mandate to be someone or something is also found in the Bible. God commands us to be good, to be righteous. We ought to do the right thing. We ought not to murder. We ought to respect our parents. We ought not envy or lie. Jesus ups the ante when he says, "Be perfect, therefore, as your father in heaven is perfect" (Matthew 5:48). Christians call these commands "the Law." By revealing how short we fall, the Law shows us who we are. It gives us an identity as sinners.

a) St. Paul claims the Law is written on the heart (Romans 2), that everyone, regardless of his or her religious beliefs, has some internal voice that says, "You must be…," fill in the blank – thin, popular, wealthy, successful. Or "You must *not* be… different, mediocre, "super."

i) The Law may sound bad or cruel, but it actually isn't. After all, murder is terrible. Adultery tears up families and destroys children. These "oughts" and "shoulds" are not arbitrary; they are right and good.

b) The Law of God judges human beings for who they are on the inside and for what they do on the outside. The Law judges our internal and external lives, our inherited givens that we can and cannot control. And for good reason. Human beings are helplessly self-centered and hurt and defensive – and this is not okay, with other people or with God.

2) In the world of *The Incredibles*, identity is mandated as well. The threat of litigation prevents superheroes from acting as superheroes and using their superpowers. There is a strict law – on the government books – that forbids these people from being themselves. "Being Super" is not right or good or legally permissible.

   a) In a sense, the prohibition of superpowers in the movie makes some sense. "Supers" cause an incredible amount of physical damage. They make their own laws. They play God.

3) But what happens in *The Incredibles* is incredibly (!) revealing. The command to be a certain way, both as an external command (Mr. and Mrs. Incredible) and an internal one (Syndrome), does not produce goodness. It produces deceit and depression in one case, control and fear in another and straight-up evil in the other.

   a) Does being told to do something make you able to do it? Does being commanded to be a certain way give you the ability to transform? Clearly it does not.

   b) This coheres with the Biblical account, which tells us, counter-intuitively, that the Law produces its opposite. *"The Law was added so that the trespass might increase"* (Romans 5:20a). That the command to be a certain way or do a certain thing, regardless of how good or right that thing or way is, creates rebellion and resentment.

   c) The human propensity to maintain and control one's own identity at all costs is called sin. To look to oneself as the arbiter of identity is slavery. To make a good thing into an ultimate thing is called idolatry.

What is the solution? What does this mean for us today?

1) Mr. Incredible illustrates that affirmation of who we are at our best may energize us to the core, but it is not the whole story. Freedom from the command to be a certain way is essential, but is it really freedom if it is so circumstantial? AKA, if it is dependent on lavish missions on secret islands?

2) Syndrome illustrates that finding our worth in our abilities is a dead-end street. It's a never-ending chase that often leads to desperation and destruction. To define yourself in reaction to someone or something is just as confining as conforming.

3) Part of the answer lies with Elastigirl, whose love for her husband and children is clearly not dependent on their abilities or attributes. In fact, this love trumps her need to control. Their worthiness, in her eyes, is not based on performance – it is based on her love for them. When true crisis hits, her doing flows from her being, not vice versa. In this sense, she functions as the God character, and as her husband and children come to understand her unswerving love for them, they naturally grow into their "real" identities.

   a) The great insight of the Bible, echoed in *The Incredibles*, is that identity comes from outside of us, not from within. Through his death and resurrection, Jesus imputes to us his identity. There is no more trying. Our ultimate value is his value, and it is not something that can be compromised or diminished. There is no more approval to attain. And since our ultimate identity does not have to do with *our* abilities or disabilities, self-congratulation and self-satisfaction have no place.

   b) Read the story of the conversion of Saul/Paul in Acts chapter 9. Jesus gives him a new name! Freedom from his self-created identity (Phillipians 3:3-11).

4) We are free, like Dash and Violet at the end of the film, to be ourselves, secure in the love we have been shown. Like Mr. Incredible, when confronted with the consequences of self-generated identity, we can give up. We can even lay claim to the same freedom that gives him new life in the film, minus any connection to our performance. Our identities in Christ, are connected only to the love of God, which is now and forever.

Discussion and Primer Questions

1. What superpower would you want and why?

2. Have you ever felt that you had to be a certain person in order to gain approval or love? What was it like?

3. When have you felt best about yourself? Where do you find your value? Which character do you identify with most?

4. What would life be like as a "human being" rather than a "human doing"?

UP!: **Guilt, Absolution and a Whole Lot of Balloons**

Synopsis

Up! is the story of an elderly man named Carl Fredrickson and his quest to fulfill an old promise to take his late wife Ellie on a trip to exotic Paradise Falls. When he is ordered by a judge to leave his beloved house to make room for a new development, Carl resolves to go to Paradise Falls by attaching thousands of balloons to his house. The film depicts his very eventful journey. Carl is accompanied by three unwanted travel companions: a boy named Russell, a dog named Dug, and a female bird named Kevin, all of whom only seem to get between Carl and his goal of reaching the Falls.

It should be said that the movie as a whole is unconcerned with Russell, Dug and Kevin in relation to Carl's character development. They are each likable characters, but their likability is not enough to dissuade Carl from his prime objective. The directors themselves called Kevin a "MacGuffin," that is, something which drives the story but has no impact on the real plot. Though she only appears in the first twenty minutes of the movie, Ellie is by far the most important character in the film.

Play 2:44 to 11:40

Introduction

Carl and his wife Ellie saved money their entire lives to go to Paradise Falls. Each time they planned the trip, life disrupted their impending adventure. The truck would have a flat tire, Carl would break his leg, or a tree would fall on their house. When they finally have enough money to make the trip, Ellie's health has declined too much. She dies without ever seeing the Falls.

The Square

1) After Ellie's death, Carl shuts himself off from the world. Ellie had made his life colorful and vibrant, but without her, Carl becomes bitter and set in his ways.

    a) Carl's character can be described exactly by how he looks: a square. His glasses are square, his head is square, his body is square, his fingers are square, his alarm clock and lamp are both square. As a geometric shape, squares do not move very easily. The same is true for Carl. He has the same routine everyday and stubbornly refuses to sell his house. His door has five locks on it.

    b) If Carl is square, Ellie was round. She was a true adventurer with an unbridled spirit. Ellie's enthusiasm was able to lure Carl out of his shell to be spontaneous and take risks. Ellie's death freezes Carl in time. The house itself remains in the same order as when she died. Instead of the optimistic adventurer, he has become closed off to other people and the world. He lives his life always looking backward at what might have been.

2) Faced with the prospect of forced eviction, Carl sets off for Paradise Falls, house in tow, to fulfill Ellie's and his lifelong dream of visiting the Falls.

a) It is clear from the outset that this trip is a quest to appease the memory of his deceased wife. It is an attempt to recapture her.

b) The house itself represents Ellie and her continued presence in his life. Carl believes that if he can just get the house (figuratively, Ellie) to the Falls, he will no longer be a disappointment in her eyes. He wants to become, once again, the man she married. Carl must atone for his failure to keep his promise. The house is so important to Carl that he is willing to sacrifice Russell, Dug, Kevin, and the life of Kevin's babies to keep it intact.

Ellie's Message from the Grave – Play 1:10.23-1:13.37

1) Carl has finally reached the Falls and achieved what he set out to do, yet he still feels empty. He puts his house back together, sits down to relax and enjoy the peace he so desires. The hero's miraculous feat isn't as fulfilling as he thought it would be. In his moment of triumph, he can only think of his past disappointment.

a) As he turns each page in Ellie's adventure book he is still reminded of her absence and his failure. He tearfully looks upward as if searching for a sign that he has done well. We then unexpectedly find out that Ellie finished her adventure book.

i) Instead of blank pages, Carl finds a scrapbook telling the story of their life together. Carl was not a disappointment to Ellie; she was delighted with him. Her message was not one of condemnation, but "Thanks for the adventure – now go have a new one! Love, Ellie."

b) Ellie's message to Carl in that moment is a declaration of *absolution*. Practically speaking, Carl was guilty. He felt like he had failed Ellie, and her memory was a perpetual judgment of his inadequacy. But Ellie expunges Carl's broken promise and rewrites the past as an endless adventure with the love of her life. So far as Ellie was concerned, Carl was the adventurer he always wanted to be!

The New Adventure – Play from 1:13.37 to 1:15.26

1) Everything Must Go!

   a) What does Carl do without the burden of his regret? He cleans house! He lets go of his quest to live by Paradise Falls and resolves to go save Kevin. He abandons all of the possessions he has held so tightly. In the end, he even lets go of the house itself. Carl's old life has passed away. Everything which defined who he was is thrown into a pile (with a touch of reverence by setting the chairs side by side).

   b) Carl is reborn and given a newfound enthusiasm for life. When Carl puts on Russell's merit badge sash he is no longer an old man, but resembles an action hero. His old walking cane becomes a weapon to fight off Charles Muntz. Even the house seems to fly with a new vigor.

2) The Birth of Love and Reconciliation.

   a) Carl's new adventure will not be undertaken alone. While he spent the majority of the movie bemoaning the presence of other people, he now gladly accepts the title of Dug's new master. Instead of shutting the world out, Carl is now freed to love his unexpected new family. The movie ends with Carl giving Russell the Ellie badge – the highest honor he can bestow. Russell finds the father he needs and Carl finds the son he never had.

Absolution and the Bible

1) Isaiah 65:16-17: *"Whoever invokes a blessing in the land will do so by the God of truth; he who takes an oath in the land will swear by the God of truth. For the past troubles will be forgotten and hidden from my eyes. Behold, I will create new heavens and a new earth. The former things will not be remembered, nor will they come to mind."*

   a) Isaiah is given a vision of a time when our past, with all its failures and sorrows, will not be remembered by either God or us. Isaiah sees a time when God's blessing will overcome our troubles. He sees at a distance what God has accomplished in Christ.

   b) Because Jesus bore in himself the penalty of the past, God has remade reality as we know it into a new thing which is not determined by the weight of our regrets, but by a fresh newness. Our old life of regret, extinguished hopes, wearied efforts, and past wounds is taken away. Like Ellie's message to Carl, we are absolved of our checkered histories and given the freedom of a new adventure!

   c) Forgiveness of sin and reconciliation is so overwhelming, that Isaiah likens it to the coming an entirely new world. Forgiveness is more than a doorway through which to pass. Instead, as it did with Carl, it triggers the radical reorientation of one's life.

      i) The wounds of our past are no longer the source of life's dysfunction and fear; in fact, our healed wounds become the wellspring of creativity and spontaneous love.

Discussion and Primer Questions

1. What promise have you made that you couldn't/haven't kept? What are the areas or situations, even trivial ones, in your life where you feel guilty? That you have dreams about?

2. If a picture book was kept of your life (like Ellie's), what adventures would you have in it? What adventures would you intentionally leave out?

3. Do you ever feel like you're not good enough or that you've failed? Who do you feel is disappointed with you?

4. Has anyone ever tried to make amends with you out of the blue? Or have you tried yourself? What was it like?

Monsters, Inc.: **Fear and Love (and Fur) in Monstropolis**

Synopsis

Monsters, Inc. is about two monsters, Sully and Mike, who work at the factory of the Monsters, Inc company. Together, with a host of other monsters, Sully, Mike, and one of the villains, Randall, work to collect "screams" from children by visiting their rooms at night. The louder the screams, the more energy they collect. These screams are converted to energy which powers the city of Monstropolis. One day at the factory, Sully and Mike encounter a little girl, "Boo," who has snuck into the monster world from the human world via her closet door. In Monstropolis, human children are considered a possibly fatal health risk. Sully and Mike discover this is false, and subsequently develop affection for Boo. They then spend the rest of the movie trying to get her back to her world, keeping her safe from the evil intentions of Randall and Mr. Waternoose, CEO of Monsters, Inc. During the process of trying to get Boo home safely, Sully discovers Boo's laughter is ten times more powerful than her screams. After Sully and Mike defeat Randall and Mr. Waternoose, Monsters, Inc., changes from a "scare" factory to a "laugh factory."

Play 1:32 to 6:59

Introduction

One of the major themes of *Monsters, Inc* is the relationship between love and fear. Not saccharine love, the film deals more with deeper, heart satiating, other-worldly love: the one-way love of the Gospel message, of the *lover* loving the *unlovable*. It is the kind of love that seeks someone out who is incapable of reciprocating or responding to that love; the kind of love that depends solely on the person who loves, rather than the person being loved; the kind of love that truly quiets fear. Some would call this grace.

Boo and Sully – Play 31:04 to 34:24

1) Sully is a monster whose understanding of himself is wrapped up with being as frightening as possible, AKA the top "scarer." He does not find his value in earning others' approval, he gets it from earning their repulsion.

    a) The relationship between monsters and children, from the outset, is one defined by fear, not love. Monsters are the frightening ones, children the frightened ones. Love does not enter the equation.

        i) Children are commonly afraid of the dark and of monsters. They are afraid of the dark because it represents the unknown. They are afraid of monsters because they threaten their safety and security. Adults are the same way!

        ii) Fear makes adults defensive and controlling. Children simply scream. It's a more directly emotional and physical reaction. Perhaps a healthier one?

            (1) As the movie rightly suggests, fear is powerful fuel. It motivates and generates a great many of our actions and plans. But is it enough? Like

the residents of Monstropolis, people who are "running on fear" (i.e. all of us) are by definition afraid that the fuel will run out. So we find new things to be afraid of...

b) The irony, of course, is that the relationship between Sully and Boo gets flipped: Sully becomes deathly afraid of Boo, and Boo is delighted by Sully. Sully firmly believes that Boo is a danger to his well-being.

2) Boo is a sweet and innocent child, and very much the victim in this equation. Yet she sees Sully not as the fearsome monster he is, but as an invitingly adorable "kitty." On one level, she mistakes him for something that he is not, and treats him accordingly. As only children can do, she grows to love him extraordinarily quickly, even though he does everything in his power to get rid of her.

a) Sully (a monster!) is lovable simply because Boo has deemed him so, not because of any attribute or quality. Boo doesn't seem to expect to reciprocate; she just loves him. There is no reason for it; love that requires a reason is conditional, and not love at all.

i) Boo's affection is not just directed at someone who has shown no evidence of being able to return it, but someone who has shown consistent evidence of working *against* it – Sully is a perpetrator, in other words, not a fellow victim. His life is based on victimizing small children, making them feel scared and alone, i.e. unloved.

Can a Monster Change its Spots?

1) The rest of the movie illustrates the transformative power of Boo's love for Sully. It causes him to have a change of heart. Fear, both of Boo and as a defining characteristic, is slowly transformed into love. In other words, love acts a stronger and

more powerful fuel. Concretely, Boo's love for Sully prompts him to reconsider both his traditions (being afraid of human children) and his identity (is he really a scary monster?).

a) Sully soon finds himself acting uncharacteristically, risking everything – himself, his best friend, his job – to keep this child safe; even if it means that he needs to cut off all contact with her. He willingly sends her home to her room and shreds the door, disconnecting them forever.

2) Boo's love for Sully also has enormous ramifications on the world around them. It sets in motion a course of events that changes the entire monster universe.

a) Underlining the central dynamic of the film, the "Scare Floor" becomes a "Laugh Floor." Instead of living with the constant threat of a scare shortage, the town now has an abundance of electricity. Love is more powerful than intimidation and fear; it has the power to change the world.

3) Boo's love also has an impact on Sully's best friend, Mike. Mike begins the movie as an uninvolved bystander to the relationship between Boo and Sully. Boo is a problem that needs to be solved, not the object of love. Much of the film finds Mike going to absurd (and comic) lengths to manage the situation. He is a nervous worrywart, whose attempts to influence the drama actually end up hurting the person he loves most, his girlfriend Celia.

a) When Mike sees that Sully is willing to sacrifice everything for Boo, he is inspired to follow his lead. Mike no longer fears losing his job, his fame, his lifestyle or his love interest. He stops protesting (and micro-managing) and instead comes willingly to Sully's aid to save Boo. Control and love are often opposing forces. At least, they tend to produce opposite results.

Love and Fear in the Bible – Play 1:23:34 to 1:25:00

1) Sully and Mike's transformation from frightening, fearful, and controlling monsters to sacrificially loving ones is a dynamic mirrored in the New Testament. The power of love to destroy fear is one of its central themes.

   a) 1 John 4:18-19: *"There is no fear in love. But perfect love drives out fear, because fear has to do with punishment. The one who fears is not made perfect in love. We love because he first loved us."*

2) The film could have ended with happy, well-adjusted monsters making happy, well-adjusted kids even happier, but it doesn't. Indeed, one of the closing scenes in particular separates *Monsters, Inc.*, from other "feel-good" movies: Mike opens his palms to show Sully that his hands have been wounded by the wood of the doors he has dug through. It may be a stretch, but the imagery is there: Jesus and his cross, the ultimate source of love.

   a) When Christ died on the cross, he took on the burden of human sin. He took on our most justifiable fears: those of death, of judgment and of abandonment. He redeems our fears and replaces them with promises: the promise not only of eternal life, but the promise that the judgment of God has been satisfied (there is no more), and that he will never leave us.

3) We are not capable of drumming up this kind of unconditional love – our fear is too powerful to be overcome. We must receive it; and we can only receive it from, in, and through the one who died on a cross because he loved us.

   i) 1 John 4:10: *"This is love: not that we loved God, but that he loved us and sent his Son as an atoning sacrifice for our sins."*

ii) Because God loved us, we love him. We are not the starting point. And because we love him, we can love others even when they are still "monsters" (cf. Romans 5:7-8).

4) Real love begins with the beloved-ness, i.e. God's love for us as revealed in Jesus. As a result of his life and death, like the woman caught in adultery (John 8:2-11), we are forgiven, justified, righteous, not condemned, unworthy of death, and lovable. We have not earned it. As it did for Sully, this radically alters how we see ourselves and others. We may feel fear, we may act on it, but it is only that: a feeling. Not a reality. And that makes all the difference.

Discussion and Primer Questions

1. What were you afraid of as a child? Monsters? The dark? How did you get over that fear? What are you afraid of now?

2. Why does Boo find Sully so funny? Is she fearless or is she simply afraid of other things? If so, what are they?

3. Are there any personal traditions of yours that could use a Sully-like makeover? Where in your life are you motivated predominantly by fear? Or better, where are you not motivated by fear?

4. Have you ever been loved when you felt unlovable? How did you react?

Finding Nemo and Finding Freedom: Only the Losers Win

Synopsis

The film begins on the ocean floor, where Nemo, a clownfish, is about to leave for his first day of school. His father, Marlin, is worried that Nemo might not be ready. When Nemo was still an egg, he and a hundred of his brothers and sisters were attacked by a barracuda. Everyone besides Nemo and his father, including his mother and all of the other eggs, was killed. Wracked with guilt, Marlin promised never to let anything happen to Nemo. Marlin's overprotection leads to a conflict with Nemo, which results in Nemo's capture by a diver. The film depicts Marlin's journey (accompanied by the absent-minded Dory) to find Nemo and return to his ocean home.

Introduction

Finding Nemo is the story of humanity, told using fish. It takes us through the standard narrative arc of human experience: we try to direct the outcome of our lives, yet this struggle is counterproductive, and we fail to achieve what we want. What we ultimately need often turns out to be the very opposite of what we initially pursued.

Marlin's Burden – Play 0:30 to 14:30

1) When we first meet Marlin, he is bursting with enthusiasm for life. He loves Coral and eagerly awaits the birth of their 100 larvae. Marlin has just bought a new sea anemone (house) with a fantastic view of the ocean, despite its somewhat dangerous location next to the "drop-off," an underwater cliff which opens up to ocean's depths. Yet, Marlin's joy for life is suddenly extinguished by a violent barracuda, which kills his wife and all but one of his larva. In his grief, Marlin becomes a paranoid and fearful fish.

   a) After the death of his wife, Marlin vows that nothing will ever happen to his only surviving son, Nemo. Understandably, Marlin becomes a burdensome and overprotective parent. The one thing Nemo is told to remember about the ocean is that it's not safe. Marlin consistently curbs Nemo's adventurous spirit. As Nemo and Marlin swim together, Marlin is compensates for Nemo's damaged little fin. Instead of joining with the fish his age when they get to school, Marlin suggests that Nemo play on the sponge beds with the infants! Everything in the ocean is a threat to his and Nemo's well-being.

      i) Marlin is a parent motivated by fear. He seeks to minimize every risk and prevent every foreseeable negative outcome. Every new situation provides new opportunities for danger. Marlin lives in a perpetual state of anxiety, yet the feeling of being in control provides for Marlin the only possibility of peace and security.

         (1) It's not that Marlin shouldn't be a protective parent. Caring for one's children is undeniably good! When Nemo is carried off by the diver it is this protective instinct which heroically sends him across the world. Yet Marlin is protective not for Nemo's sake; he is protective for his own sake. He has staked his entire life on avoiding danger by means of control. It is

Marlin versus the world and no one is there to help him. Marlin thinks that he personally must (and can) keep Nemo from dying.

(2) Marlin's attempts to control Nemo are counter-productive. His efforts to protect Nemo have made Nemo rather resentful of his dad. While his constant guidance is meant to be helpful and loving, it is unavoidably received by Nemo as criticism. Nemo defiantly ventures to assert his freedom and display his swimming ability. Marlin has gripped life so fiercely that it slips through his fingers.

Only the Losers Win

Set up: Marlin, joined by the absent-minded Dory, has set off after Nemo, who they believe has been taken to "P. Sherman, 42 Wallaby Way, Sydney." After numerous set-backs, they are lost and unsure what to do next.

Play 1:04:57 to 1:06:38 and 1:08:30 to 1:13:40

1) This clip shows a real turning point of the movie for Marlin. In this impossible situation he is faced with two options. Either Marlin can hold onto the taste bud *or* he can let go and drop into the back of the whale's throat.

   a) Holding onto the taste bud seems to be the safest, most secure option. He knows he can hold onto the taste bud. Maybe he can outlast the whale's patience? Maybe he can find a way past the whale's bushy teeth (baleen)?

   b) The second option doesn't seem to be all that attractive. His traveling companion Dory claims that she can speak whale and insists that Marlin should let go and drop into the back of the whale's throat. Yet Dory hasn't proven herself to be all that reliable. It's her fault they were swallowed in the first place! And why should Marlin trust the whale? Don't whales eat fish?

i)   These straightforward alternatives symbolize for Marlin two different ways of living life: holding on and letting go.

   (1)   Up until this point, all Marlin has been doing is "holding on" – to Nemo, security, familiarity, and finally this taste bud. And despite his best efforts, this approach has produced the exact opposite of what he wants. Holding on has left him isolated from the rest of the reef, it has driven away his son, and led him into his current life-threatening situation. The decision to let go seems like a worse alternative than the first option. It would mean risking his security for the highly uncertain possibility that things might turn out better. If Marlin stays in the mouth, he'll die. He doesn't know that if he lets go, if he accepts his death, he'll be blown out the blow-hole (resurrected).

   (2)   We tend to think that holding on, AKA working hard, managing risks, doing what is expected of us, will bring our life stability. So the word to "go to the back of the throat" or "give up" can only heard as a death sentence. We think that if we can just hold on for a little longer, we might eventually get out by our own effort. We think that we must argue and struggle to get what we want, no matter what the costs. If we don't fight for what we want no one else will. If we could just try a little harder, things will be better. Right?

2)   Marlin falls victim to the universal human error: calling a bad thing (hard work) "good" and a good thing (death) "bad."

a) The great Protestant Reformer Martin Luther wrote: "Although the works of man always appear attractive and good they are nevertheless likely to be mortal sins. Although the works of God always seem unattractive and appear evil, they are nevertheless really eternal merits."

   i) Letting go and giving up may seem unattractive or even irresponsible, but it may in fact be the only way forward. While laboring for what you want, expressed here in the form of vigilant parenting, may appear attractive and good, it nevertheless can accomplish the opposite of what is intended: it can drive your children away.

   ii) Marlin looks probable death in the face and is forced into a world of uncertainty. Life is not found through holding on to what seems secure or pushing toward your goals, but through letting go! Or more precisely, being made to give up. God overwhelms our controlling natures. It is in this death, painful and frightening as it is, that we are reborn. It is Marlin's succumbing to death that enables him to be reborn as a man (fish) who is able to love his son, rather than restrict him. This is an enormously hopeful message to those who are struggling and suffering.

Death and Resurrection in the Bible

1) Mark 8:34-37: "*Then he called the crowd to him along with his disciples and said: 'If anyone would come after me, he must deny himself and take up his cross and follow me. For whoever wants to save his life will lose it, but whoever loses his life for me and for the gospel will save it. What good is it for a man to gain the whole world, yet forfeit his soul? Or what can a man give in exchange for his soul?'*"

   a) True Christian discipleship is not about a difficult or meritorious to-do list. It is not about following Jesus as he lived. It's about following Jesus as he died. Discipleship often looks like a person giving up on their hopes, letting go of their pride, and succumbing to the reality of death. It looks like being crushed by life into a position where one can truly see God at work. You don't have to succeed to get ahead! Rather, God is found in failure and weakness.

2) Jesus admonishes his hearers *not* to try to save their lives. It is the very preservation of life that he likens to "gaining the whole world." The primary obstacles between us and God are not our vices, but the very "good" things we work toward and are holding onto. They are our hopes and dreams, the places where we feel the most secure.

a) Jesus here presents the paradox of God and humanity: true life is only found through its opposite form, namely death. The way out of our trouble isn't by fighting through it, but by letting go of control. "He who loses his life will save it."

i) Romans 6:10-11: *"The death [Jesus] died, he died to sin once for all; but the life he lives, he lives to God. In the same way, count yourselves dead to sin but alive to God in Christ Jesus."*

b) The good news of the Gospel is that Jesus "let go" of everything for the sake of men and women who often find themselves unable to let go of the very things that are killing them. Like Marlin, we rarely relinquish control by willpower alone. Instead, we "let go" when we are grabbed by something greater: God himself. This is very good news for those of us that find ourselves paralyzed by fear or anger or impossible circumstances. God saves those who cannot save themselves, and brings life out of death.

Post Script: The Wondrous Story of Life!

In *Finding Nemo* we are introduced to an oceanic world which begs for exploration. It is certainly a dangerous place—in every case, the objects of Marlin's fears are all real. The sharks, jellyfish, deep sea monster, whale, fishermen and pelicans all seem to threaten Marlin and Nemo's lives. Yet for every threat we also find marvelous beauty and elegance. Instead of cowering in the face of threats like Marlin, the movie suggests when our fear has been quenched, we live with Nemo's childlike enthusiasm that sees humor, awe, and creativity at every turn. Though we never know what is going to happen next, we find that greeting the world with open arms is worth the risk.

Discussion and Primer Questions

1. Why is it so easy to fall into a pattern of control and self-reliance?

2. Have you ever met someone like Marlin? Have you ever acted like Marlin (i.e., as a control freak)? How did those around you react? How did it affect you?

3. Why would God require us to "take up our cross" if we want to follow him?

4. What kinds of "good things" do you hold on to that might prevent you from letting go?

Cars: **The Loneliness of a Short-Track Racecar**

Synopsis

Lightning McQueen is the new rookie racecar on the block, stealing headlines with every winning race. He's super fast and he knows it. When his pit crew ditches him, he doesn't care. He's headed to California to compete in the race that will determine who wins the treasured Piston Cup *and* become the new "spokescar" for the illustrious Dinoco company. But on his way to California, following a string of unfortunate events, Lightning McQueen finds himself on a barren stretch of road in a forgotten little town called Radiator Springs. In the midst of this misfit community of eccentric cars – who neither know nor care who McQueen is – he experiences real community and love like never before. This experience changes how McQueen sees life, leading him to a deeper understanding of the power of sacrifice.

Introduction

We have all heard the expression, "It's lonely at the top" or the 1969 song, by Henry Nilsson (performed by *Three Dog Night*) "One" with its familiar opening line: "One is the loneliest number that you'll ever do…" Whether we have sacrificed friends and family for elusive fame and fortune or have simply withdrawn from others to the safety of solitude, one is and always will be a very lonely number. It's hard to love or be loved when it's only you.

Play 9:30 to 19:47

The Lone Rangers: Lightning McQueen and Doc Hudson Hornet

1) McQueen is a driven (!) individual who will stop at nothing to get everything in life. He wants success, fame, and fortune, but most of all he wants to win the Piston Cup and become the Dinoco spokescar.

   a) This ambition has isolated McQueen. His motto seems to be, "One winner, 42 losers. I eat losers for breakfast." He feels that he has outgrown his sponsorship, Rust-eze Bumper Ointment. He fires three crew chiefs, provoking his pit crew to quit on him after his last race. McQueen's ambition has even left him with no friends to whom he can bestow free tickets. It's not simply that people won't tolerate McQueen's driven personality, it's that he has pushed them all away: he works alone.

   b) McQueen uses his ambition and drive to justify everything he does. He is a car on a mission! His goals are his sole purpose for living and the measure of his worth.

2) If McQueen is alone because he is driving toward success, Doc Hudson is alone because he is driving away from his failure. Doc suffered a major crash in the final lap of the Piston Cup. When he came back, the world had moved on and he was forgotten. Doc's crash revealed to him the passing and conditional nature of success and his resulting aimlessness has left him callous and cynical.

a) The world quit on him, so he quit on the world. He retreated to the town of Radiator Springs and assumed a new identity to cover up his past. Yet this disguise has prevented Doc from truly giving of himself to the residents of the town. They barely know anything about him. By his own guarded nature, Doc is alone.

   i) We have all been alone either intentionally (alienating others, like McQueen) or unintentionally (retreating or keeping ourselves closed off from others out of protection, like Doc). Either way, we often feel alone.

The Birth of Love – Play 57:56 to 1:02:40 and 1:09:36 to 1:11:30

1) McQueen is not left alone for long. Something external draws him out of himself and into community. Someone else's love has a dramatic effect on him.

   a) To McQueen, Mater, the old-fashioned tow truck, is a persistent nuisance. Mater claims to be the backward driving world champion. McQueen is embarrassed by Mater and would rather not be around him. Yet, Mater chooses McQueen as his best friend. Mater loves Lightning McQueen for absolutely no reason but "just because."

   b) Like Sally before him, McQueen encounters a love in Radiator Springs that overcomes the ambition that marked his prior life. This community takes him in like one of their own. For McQueen, the town of Radiator Springs becomes a place with true friends and a true family who love him; and it's a love that is neither merited by achievements nor conditioned by failures. Mater, Ramon, Flo, and Sally welcome him with no strings attached. It is a town of misfits and rejects where everyone belongs.

      i) Doc Hudson observes how the town has taken to McQueen and is inspired to step out of the shadows and reveal his true identity. He sees how much

McQueen's presence has enlivened the town and how dead the town is after McQueen leaves.

The New Lightning McQueen – Play 1:32:30 to 1:44:02

1) McQueen's newfound joy reorients him completely. Instead of the self-aggrandizing "need for speed," he now thinks only of his new family in Radiator Springs. Moreover, the new Lightning McQueen does not love in a superficial way; he loves in a sacrificial way.

   a) After finishing repairing the road he destroyed, McQueen stays an extra day in Radiator Springs to lovingly serve everyone in the town. As the first customer in years, he buys new tires, a new paint job, new organic fuel, and new bumper stickers. For Sally, he renovates the town's neon lights so she can see it as it was in its heyday. Lightning McQueen has been transformed both figuratively and literally.

   b) In the final Piston Cup race, a few feet before crossing the finish line and achieving his dream of winning, McQueen slams on his breaks. A moment later Chick goes whizzing by and celebrates his win. Meanwhile, McQueen, still not having crossed the finish line, backs-up and goes to The King's side. But it's not to see if The King is okay; it's to help The King across the finish line, to allow him the dignity of finishing his last race. McQueen sacrifices his career (he will even sacrifice the Dinoco spokescar slot to remain loyal to Rust-eze) and comes in not second but dead last.

      (1) Through his sacrifice, McQueen reverses the course of history. He breaks the seemingly endless cycle of discarding heroes who are past their prime. While Doc was trampled upon by the next generation of racecars, The King is honored by the rookie McQueen's sacrifice.

Sin as Isolation in the Bible

1) The Bible often talks about how we are separated from God, alienated from him because of sin. In the book of Colossians, Paul writes, *"Once you were alienated from God and were enemies in your minds because of your evil behavior"* (1:21). The Old Testament, too, contains references to the Israelites being exiled because of their sinful ways. Like McQueen, our desires have led us away from both people and God.

   a) If we zoom out to the wider context surrounding Col. 1:21, Paul has a bigger message to tell us: *"For God was pleased to have all his fullness dwell in him, and through him to reconcile to himself all things, whether things on earth or things in heaven, by making peace through his blood, shed on the cross. Once you were alienated from God and were enemies in your minds because of your evil behavior. But now he has reconciled you by Christ's physical body through death to present you holy in his sight, without blemish and free from accusation"* (Col. 1:19-22).

   b) Through the sacrifice of Jesus Christ on the cross, we, by faith, are no longer alienated from God, no longer alone, but are in communion with God himself. This (one-way) love of Christ for us pours into us and, subsequently, out of us toward others.

   c) Our achievements and our failures no longer define who we are. God loves us as we are, not as we should be, thus making room for true and real transformation.

Post-Script: The Church of Radiator Springs

At its best, the church is a community drawn together by this one-way love, flowing from God to sinner to neighbor. It is a community of misfits that is, through the Spirit, birthed by that love and empowered for loving service in the world.

Discussion and Primer Questions

1. When have you felt most lonely? Are there specific triggers, like certain places or times of day?

2. How did that loneliness dissipate? Did it?

3. What are your ambitions? Who is the most ambitious person you know? What are they like?

4. Have you ever been befriended by someone in spite of your actions, attitudes, etc? Better yet, have you ever de-friended someone because of theirs?

Ratatouille: **Passion, Purpose and Pest-Control**

Synopsis

A French rat named Remy dreams of becoming a great chef despite his family's wishes and the obvious problem of being a rat in a decidedly rodent-phobic profession. When fate places Remy in the sewers of Paris, he finds himself ideally situated beneath a restaurant made famous by his culinary hero, Auguste Gusteau. Despite the dangers of being an unlikely – and unwanted – visitor in the kitchen of a gourmet restaurant, Remy's passion for cooking soon sets into motion a rat race that turns Paris upside down.

Introduction

Ratatouille is a dense film, with many interweaving plotlines and themes. We will focus on two aspects: 1. The relationship of Remy to himself (or Remy's relationship to imaginary Gusteau) and 2. The relationships of Remy to Linguini. There are plenty of other conflicts worth speaking about (Skinner vs. Remy, Ego vs. Gusteau).

Play 0:30 to 10:00

Remy's Internal Struggle

1) Remy is a rat, but dreams about being a chef. Unlike his fellow rats, he appreciates gourmet food and cooking. He feels that his purpose is to cook. This is, of course, at odds with his rat-ness: rats and kitchens are mutually exclusive.

    a) Remy's internal struggle has to do with the question of purpose which goes hand-in-hand with the question of identity. "What should I do with my life? Why am I here? What will make me happy and fulfilled?" We all ask these questions – they are universal. The two competing answers to these questions in the film, that is the depiction of Remy's internal struggle over his purpose, come from his father on one side, and the ghost of Gusteau on the other.

        i) Remy's father: A rat is a rat. Accept your biological givens. Contributing to the good of the pack is a rat's purpose, and more important than the good of the individual.

        ii) Ghost Gusteau is the embodiment of what Remy has internalized from watching Gusteau on TV and reading his book, combined with his own deeply felt passion. The voice of Remy's "inner-cook." Remy *must* pursue his dreams, no matter what. There is nothing to be afraid of. Gusteau says: *"Great cooking is not for the faint of heart. You must be imaginative, strong-hearted. You must try things that may not work. You must not let anyone define your limits because of where you come from. Your only limit is your soul. What I say is true: anyone can cook, but only the fearless can be great!"* Cooking itself is what matters, the gift, the art of it, with no mention of the rewards it brings.

b) The movie advocates a middle-ground between these two opposing voices: Remy's pursuit of his dream being both courageous (risking his own life for his art) *and* self-seeking (putting the rest of the pack at risk).

    i) Were the filmmakers to side solely with Ghost Gusteau's position, the message of the movie would be a familiar one: if you can just figure out your purpose, what you're good at, what your gifts are, you will be happy. Which, in reality, is an enormous burden.

    ii) But were they solely to endorse Remy's father, the filmmakers would be denying the beauty and value of God-given passions and gifts, implying that they should be suppressed in service of the larger community. That perspective is dreary - it not only creates resentment in those being suppressed (*ergo*, a less functional community), life becomes an endless litany of what "needs" to be done. "Wants" are viewed as a threat.

        (1) The truth is that a purpose, in and of itself, is not a bad thing. Passions are precious and rare. Everyone is created differently. Yet the human tendency is to take a gift and turn it into a commodity, a means for self-aggrandizement. What begins as a simple passion consumes us, even to the point of harming ourselves and those around us!

            (a) On the roof with his brother Emile, it wasn't enough for Remy to be given a unique mushroom dish cooked by lightning – no, he needed saffron! This single misstep threatens the life of the entire colony. His father's resistance to his dream of being a cook is not irrational.

            (b) Another example of purpose running wild is the real-life Gusteau. When his restaurant loses a star, he is so distraught that he gets sick and dies of despair… Clearly his purpose as a cook had become overly intertwined with his self-worth.

c) In theological terms, the question of purpose can be both Law (demand) and Gospel (promise).

   i) Law: "If I can just figure out what I'm good at, I'll be happy. My life will be fulfilled." That can be a tortuous burden to live under. What if you get it wrong? You will constantly second-guess yourself. Or what if you lose your gift?

   ii) Gospel: We have God-given gifts. Augustine famously wrote, "Love God and do what you will." To someone who has suppressed their passion, the encouragement to try, to not be afraid, would be heard as freedom and love.

   (1) In the next clip, we will see how Remy's struggle plays out.

The Remy-Linguini Relationship

1) The relationship revolves around the dynamic of collaboration and the question of credit. The physical comedy is a brilliant and amusing outworking of their sometimes conflicted partnership.

2) Their collaboration is born of humility: Remy is willing not to get credit for his cooking – just to create is enough. And Linguini is willing to be wielded like a puppet so that he can keep a job. They need each other. And they trust each other.

   a) Remy's gift (and Linguini's as well) does not exist in a vacuum. He needs other people. He needs help from the outside.

b) The success of their collaboration breeds resentment. Before credit had to be claimed, there was no relational strife. Their success was a form of fulfilling the Law, of meeting the standard of the outside world, which (almost automatically) produced self-righteousness and entitlement. In other words, as we'll see in the press conference scene, the fame goes to their heads. Remy feels slighted and unappreciated, while Linguini feels put upon and taken for granted. They each want the credit and the glory!

  i) This is a poisonous dynamic in any relationship: romantic, professional, familial. It is why successful rock bands break up.

c) Let's take a look at how these two relationships are resolved. Set up: *Linguini has been promoted to full-cook status and has begun a romantic relationship with his colleague Collette, who doesn't know about Remy. The restaurant has been getting its best reviews since Gusteau's death, piquing the interest of renowned but scary food critic Anton Ego. Remy has just made public that Linguini is actually Gusteau's son, and therefore the heir of the restaurant, much to the chagrin of head-chef Skinner.*

Play climax from 1:17:48 to 1:41:00

In Reverse Order: Linguini-Remy

1) Their disagreements and betrayals bring them to a point of crisis, to their knees. The "wages of sin" is the death of their relationship. Their self-seeking and fearful behavior leads directly to their break-up.

a) Without one another, they recognize their dependence and are humbled by it. They relinquish their claims of credit. They are both the subjects and objects of this development. That is, while the defeat is a result of their own actions, it also happens to them.

b) The renewed humility creates the space for love, which results in honesty, courage, collaboration and creativity. Specifically, it births the selflessness, goodness, and inspiration that define the final meal.

    i) We grow through defeat, and more often than not, we are both the author and the victim of our defeats. The giving up precedes the victory. This is what Paul means in 2 Cor. 7:9, when he talks about sorrow leading to repentance. Suffering leads to an apology which leads to new life.

c) The selfless love achieved through (unwittingly) self-engineered defeat reaches its apex when Linguini courageously admits, "He's the reason!" Linguini says, pointing to Remy, "You've been giving me credit for his gift!"

    i) The Linguini-Remy relationship is a touching picture of what Christians mean when they talk about substitution. We point to Christ as the one who has already done everything for us. He died the death we deserve, and in return, we are given his "righteousness" or identity. We get the "credit" for his work. This is good news!

        (1) Romans 5:19: *"For just as through the disobedience of the one man the many were made sinners, so also through the obedience of the one man the many will be made righteous."*

Remy's Internal Struggle

1) When Remy's trapped in the cage, the Ghost Gusteau tells him "You know who you are" (1:27:00). Gusteau is telling him that he no longer needs to pretend, to be human or to be a rat. Remy's attempts to assert his identity, to foist his purpose on those around him, have been completely thwarted. He gives up.

a) "Why do I need to pretend?" he cries, "I'm through with pretending!" Ghost Gusteau responds, "You don't have to pretend. You never had to." His chains (the jail bars!) are self-imposed. They are an illusion. Instead, there is freedom: to do the job joyfully, yet without his self-worth being determined by it. He is a cook because he is a cook, not because he cooks. Remy is also freed to accept that he is a rat and has a place in the colony, no matter how unrefined they are.

b) "Knowing who you are" is not always the road to freedom. Because "who we are" is 1. Always mixed, both positive and negative, charitable yet self-seeking, loving yet fearful, etc. and 2. Always changing. What we enjoyed at age fifteen we seldom enjoy at thirty (except Michael Jackson's *Thriller*, of course).

c) In Christ, we are freed from the burden of having to find out who we are, of having to get that right... or else. The cross gives our attempts at fashioning a purpose for ourselves the proper perspective – i.e., they are only valuable so far as they are born of freedom. In a certain sense, Jesus died because we have failed to be who we are. We have failed to live up to our potential, to fulfill our purpose.

   i) Like Remy in the cage, we can give up on "purpose" as a means of self-fulfillment. In fact, freedom often comes to us when we have given up (or been forced to give up) our prerogatives. *"It is for freedom that Christ has set us free"* (Galatians 5:1a).

      (1) "I need to find myself in order to be happy" no longer applies in the same way. You have been found. Or like Remy as a cook, we are loved because we are loved, not because we are loveable.

      (2) Ego even "bestows" Remy with an identity as the greatest chef in Paris, at the precise point when it no longer matters (they open up a hole-in-the-wall restaurant).

ii)   Paradoxically, this kind of existential freedom often gives us the space to find a purpose. To do what we have dreamed about doing. Or to go where we feel called to go. To follow our hearts. Or not! And to do so without deference to consequences or pre-conceived notions about what we "need" to be or be doing.

(1)   As a closing image, we should be reminded of Linguini, waiting tables in the climatic sequence. It turns out that he's an incredible waiter! The same flexibility/elasticity that provided so much slapstick humor earlier is put to perfect use – as a *servant* no less. He has found a purpose.

Post Script: Ego's Conversion

Another powerful aspect of the film is Ego's conversion. If time allows, we encourage you to mention it. Probably best incorporated after the Romans quote (5:19) at the end of the second part of the Linguini-Remy discussion.

1)   Eating the ratatouille, Ego has a conversion experience. He is transported back to childhood. The tastes remind him of being taken care of as a boy by his mother. They make him feel loved. He abreacts – in a moment he is undone, his defenses penetrated – *he is born again.* Jesus says, we must become like children (Matt. 18:3).

a)   Nazareth principle: Good things coming from unexpected places. Who would expect the savior of the world to be a first-century peasant from a backwater town?

b)   Not only is the cook unexpected, the ratatouille itself is an odd choice. Similarly, the Christian Gospel is counter-intuitive. More often than not, it hits us sideways, in our blind spot, the vulnerable and needy place. We don't expect it, so our defenses are not up. 1 Cor 1:27 *"But God chose the foolish things of the world to shame the wise; God chose the weak things of the world to shame the strong."*

c) Ego's words are the words of a converted man: "In the past, I have made no secret of my disdain for Chef Gusteau's famous motto, 'Anyone can cook.' But I realize – only now do I truly understand what he meant. Not everyone can become a great artist, but a great artist can come from *anywhere*. It is difficult to imagine more humble origins than those of the genius now cooking at Gusteau's, who is, in this critic's opinion, nothing less than the finest chef in France."

Discussion and Primer Questions

1. Do you feel you have a purpose? If so, what is it? How did you come to find it out? Do other people have a purpose for your life?

2. Have you ever not received credit for something you did? How did you react? Have you ever received credit for something you weren't responsible for?

3. Have you ever found yourself pretending to be someone you're not?

4. What happens to Ego at the end of the film? How is he changed and what is he changed into and from?

Toy Story 1, 2 and 3: **Magic Markers and the Nobility of Belonging**

Synopsis

The *Toy Story* trilogy revolves around the adventures of a playroom full of living toys, who belong to a boy named Andy. Each installment depicts a different interruption of the playroom status quo. In *Toy Story 1* (TS1) it is the addition of the latest and greatest toy, action figure Buzz Lightyear. In *Toy Story 2* (TS2) it is the kidnapping of Woody the cowboy by a zealous toy collector. In *Toy Story 3* (TS3) it is the accidental transplantation of the toys to a new home. In each case, these interruptions prompt an adventure: In the first film, it is a quest to save Buzz from the mischievous neighbor and in the second, a daring mission to save Woody from the thief. In the third and final film, it is a "great escape" from a prison-like daycare center. But unlike most films, the climax of the plots do not involve some heroic feat to save the day, but rather the repentance, or defeat, of the main character(s).

The Nobility of Being a Toy

In each movie, Buzz and Woody learn (the hard way) about the nobility of being a toy – of being Andy's toy – a lesson which forces them to give up their illusions of grandeur. This "repentance" comes about through accepting the reality and nobility of being who they are. According to *Toy Story*, life does not consist in trying to become something important (AKA doing), but in being and in being loved.

Toy Story 1: **Just a Toy**

In TS1, Buzz is entirely delusional about who he is. He thinks he is a *real* space ranger sent to Earth to defeat Emperor Zurg. He believes that his laser is deadly and that he can fly on command. He has been given a mission from Star Command, and he is determined to fulfill it. Despite Star Command's continual silence, Woody's emphatic suggestions, and gravity, Buzz believes he is a real space ranger. This makes for a lot of clever comedy, of course. But eventually Buzz comes back down to Earth and is confronted by the obvious reality that he is simply a toy, or, as he says, "a child's play-thing."

1) **Play TS1 56:42 to 59:40**

    a) Dealing with reality on its own terms – looking at ourselves honestly with all of our inadequacies – can be unbearable. Though we can try, like Buzz, to ignore reality, its power still irrepressibly pulls on us. Yet Buzz's despair was only a momentary necessity that allowed him to see that he, as a toy, is loved by Andy and marked as his own.

        i) His insistence on asserting his "false identity" even puts the toys at great risk. Denial is more than unfortunate and misinformed, it is dangerous.

    b) At Buzz's lowest point, when he is discouraged and disillusioned, Woody (who functions as a prophet figure) tells him, "Being a toy is a whole lot better than being a space ranger. . . Look, over in that house is a kid who thinks that you are the greatest. . . you are his toy." Buzz then looks down on the sole of his boot and sees "Andy" written in permanent marker. Immediately, he springs into action. Buzz is saved from his despair through the assurance that he belongs to, and is loved by, Andy.

i) The first step to real, authentic life is to see things as they really are. If one is a toy, one is not a real space ranger. While a toy may demonstrate similarities to a real space ranger, it is not an actual space ranger. To see oneself as *just* a toy is to look at life as it really is, to see one's failures and hurt and accept them.

Toy Story 2: **The Greatest Thing Of All**

In TS2, Buzz and Woody have switched places. Andy is growing up and does not have the same amount of interest in his toys. In his absence, Woody has (understandably) forgotten the nobility of being a toy and instead is tempted to eternal fame and immortality as an exhibit in a Japanese toy museum. Woody desires greatness and the accolades of children forever. He desires their love. Yet this is not real love; it is a mirage. To be loved by everyone, and yet by no one in particular is not to be loved at all. Woody will never be held or played with again.

1) **Play TS2 1:04:04 to 1:08:08**

a) "Life's only worth living if you're being loved by a kid" In light of Andy's love for Woody, Woody gives up his desire for fame and immortality. He steps away from the certainty of the museum and in faith steps toward an uncertain life with Andy.

b) As in all the *Toy Story* films, there is a strong sense of what Jesus articulates in Luke 9:24: *"For whoever wants to save his life will lose it, but whoever loses his life for me will save it."*

2) **Play TS1 0:16 to 2:46**

   a) Real life then is found in being loved – the song in TS2 "When Somebody Loved Me" being the negative articulation – literally in the hands of Andy. Only in the hands of Andy does Woody become a real cowboy. He is a creature, not the creator. In Andy's hands Woody lassos a box, he saves Bo Peep's sheep from the wiles of one-eyed Bart, and he rides in the Wild-Wild West. In Andy's hands Woody is loved and appreciated as a real member of Woody's Roundup. Andy's loving hands make Woody and Buzz who they are designed to be.

Toy Story 3: **The Gang Goes Sunny Side Up**

In TS3, the toys again fall for a false idea of happiness and forget who they are. This time it has less to do with their identities as toys, and more to do with their identities as Andy's toys. After years of neglect, they think that Andy has discarded them, and they are presented with the seemingly perfect new home of the Sunnyside Day Care Center. Who do the toys belong to? Would the toys continue to be Andy's toys (at their own peril!), or will they choose the safety of Sunnyside?

1) **Play TS3 26:30-29:00**

   a) Woody functions again as the prophet, reminding them of who they are, how Andy has treated them in the past, and urging them to stay true, despite all the evidence to the contrary. He is the lone voice "calling out in the wilderness."

      i) And again, Woody's faith in Andy leads him to make a counter-intuitive and, by all appearances, foolish decision (see Luke 9:24).

   b) The delusion in the third film has to do not with being a space ranger, or moving to a Japanese toy museum, but in the Sunnyside Day Care Center – "everything a toy would ever want." It is not what it appears to be. The offer of love in fact turns out to be the opposite: the age-inappropriate toddlers hurt and abuse the toys. **Play 44:00 to 46:00.**

c) Lotso Huggin Bear represents the false prophet in this scenario – lying to them about who they are, and who Andy is. Lotso offers false promises of easy love and exploits the toys for his own gain. Yet, as we soon learn, his sin flows out of his own personal hurt – his (falsely) perceived abandonment by his owner.

d) Once the toys realize what's going on they "repent" – they turn around and try to escape. But this time it's not enough. The attempt is both dangerous and doomed.

2) **Play 72:00 to 84:30.** On their way to the incinerator, it looks as though they have been utterly defeated. And they have been. Their best efforts are not enough. The result of their faithlessness (and delusion) is certain death. Not just one character this time, but all of them.

a) God intervenes after all hope is lost. The toys are rescued, first by Woody (who they had denied) and then by The Claw. The crucifixion is followed by the resurrection.

b) Not only that, they are given new identities, new lives even, by Andy: toys loved by a new owner – **Play 89:00 to 93:00.** Is this a glimpse of heaven?

Being Human and the Bible

1) Ephesians 2:1-10: *"As for you, you were dead in your transgressions and sins,… gratifying the cravings of our sinful nature and following its desires and thoughts. Like the rest, we were by nature objects of wrath. But because of his great love for us, God, who is rich in mercy, made us alive with Christ even when we were dead in transgressions—it is by grace you have been saved. And God raised*

us up with Christ and seated us with him in the heavenly realms in Christ Jesus, in order that in the coming ages he might show the incomparable riches of his grace, expressed in his kindness to us in Christ Jesus. For it is by grace you have been saved, through faith—and this not from yourselves, it is the gift of God— not by works, so that no one can boast. For we are God's workmanship, created in Christ Jesus to do good works, which God prepared in advance for us to do."

a)   Just as in *Toy Story*, we must first come to see ourselves as we really are. We are just like everybody else, desiring to become someone important, to have something we can call our own. According to *Toy Story*, this takes the form of trying to be more than a toy, whether it be a space ranger or a famous museum exhibit or a donated toy. In the Ephesians passage above, Paul calls this *"gratifying the cravings of our sinful nature and following its desires and thoughts."*

    i)   The end of this trajectory is always the same—disappointment, frustration, and emptiness. But we must see ourselves first as being worthy of God's wrath and bankrupt by what we have created. We thought that if we could just have things our way then life would be better, yet we find ourselves trapped, not free (TS3).

b)   But God does not leave us alone in our despair. The death of Jesus absorbed for us the shockwave of our self-delusions. Though we are beggars, in Jesus he has given us the *"incomparable riches of his grace."* Through Christ, we have become *"God's workmanship."* Like Andy's toys, we find life when we are grasped by God. In his hands we are *"made alive"* and he has raised us *"up with Christ and seated us with him in the heavenly realms in Christ Jesus."*

    i)   Though we are *only* human, to be truly human is the greatest thing in the world. Life is only worth living if we are loved by God, if we are *his*. God's hands do not confine or restrict, but liberate and restore.

Discussion Questions

1. What was your favorite toy growing up? Why did you like it so much?

2. Woody often fears that Andy has disregarded him in favor of something else. Has it ever felt like God has disregarded you?

3. Do you know anyone who believes themselves to be different than they actually are? Why do they cling to their delusions? Have you ever been disillusioned about some trait of yours?

4. Where would you like your life to end up? What if it doesn't (hasn't!) ended the way you hoped?

For Further Reading

Gerhard Forde. *On Being a Theologian of the Cross* (Grand Rapids: Eerdmans Publishing, 1997).

Karen Paik. *To Infinity and Beyond!: The Story of Pixar Animations Studios* (San Fransisco: Chronicle Books, 2007).

David A. Price. *The Pixar Touch: The Making of a Company* (New York: Vintage Books, 2008).

Travis Prinzi. *Harry Potter & Imagination: The Way Between Two Worlds* (Zossima Press, 2008).

Paul F. M. Zahl. *Grace in Practice: A Theology of Everyday Life* (Grand Rapids: Eerdmans Publishing, 2007).

Also from Mockingbird Ministries*

The Gospel According to The Office

Grace in Addiction: What the Church Can Learn from Alcoholics Anonymous

Judgment & Love

Two Words Devotional [Teaser]

The Useful Sinner

Who Will Deliver Us? The Present Power of the Death of Christ

*To order copies of our publications, please visit www.mbird.com.

Contributors

Todd Brewer is a graduate student in theology at the University of Durham in the UK, where he and his wife Kelly currently live. He is an Episcopal priest and graduate of Trinity School for Ministry in Ambridge, PA. His favorite Pixar film is *The Incredibles*.

Lauren R. E. Larkin is a Masters student in theology and a full-time mom. She lives in Ambridge PA, with her husband, Daniel, and their two sons, Quinn and Jack. Her favorite Pixar film is a tie between *Cars* and *Monsters, Inc*.

The Rev. Nick Lannon is pastor of Grace Church Van Vorst (Episcopal) in Jersey City, NJ. He has a wife, Aya, and two children, Hazel and Patrick. His favorite Pixar film is *Ratatouille*.

Bonnie Poon Zahl is a Ph.D. student in psychology and religion at the University of Cambridge. She lives in England with her husband, Simeon, and their son, Thomas. Her favorite Pixar film is *WALL-E*, with *Monsters, Inc* a close second.

David Zahl is the executive director and founder of Mockingbird Ministries. He lives with his wife, Cate, and their son, Charlie, in Charlottesville, VA, where he also serves on the staff at Christ Episcopal Church. David's favorite Pixar movie is a toss-up between *The Incredibles* or *Toy Story 3*.

.

About Mockingbird

Mockingbird is a ministry that seeks to connect the historic truths of the Christian Gospel with the realities of everyday life in as down-to-earth a way possible. Founded in 2007, the name was inspired by the mockingbird's peculiar gift for mimicking the cries of other birds. In a similar way, we seek to repeat the message of God's grace and forgiveness. At present we do this via a variety of media, including (but not limited to) a daily weblog (mockingbirdnyc.blogspot.com), regular conferences and meetings, and an ongoing publications initiative.

For more information about Mockingbird, or details about how you can financially support this ministry, please visit our website at www.mbird.com or contact us at info@mockingbirdnyc.com.

Made in the USA
Monee, IL
15 May 2021